The Children's
DISCOVERY
BIBLE
Devotions

This book belongs to:

_____

Presented by:

_____

Date:

_____

Carla Williams
Illustrated by Drew Rose

ChariotVICTOR
PUBLISHING
A DIVISION OF COOK COMMUNICATIONS

To Granny,
Thank you for helping me discover
the joys of a daily Bible devotional
when I was young.
C. W.

Chariot Books is an imprint of ChariotVictor Publishing
A division of Cook Communications, Colorado Springs, Colorado 80918
Cook Communications, Paris, Ontario
Kingsway Communications, Eastbourne, England

THE CHILDREN'S DISCOVERY BIBLE DEVOTIONS
© 1997 by Cook Communications.

Cover and interior design by Bradley L. Lind
Art Direction by Andrea Boven
Illustrations by Drew Rose

First printing, 1997
Printed in the United States of America
01 00 99 98 97   5 4 3 2 1

Table of Contents

Introduction

*Help your child learn about God
with his or her eyes, ears, and hands!*

God created each child to learn in a different way. Some children learn best by seeing, while others need a "hands-on" experience. In *The Children's Discovery Bible Devotions* we have provided a unique but simple approach to learning Bible truths.

When using this book, keep these special features in mind:

•Each devotion is short and has a variety of activities. You can pick and choose what works best with your child.

•Each devotion focuses on one specific, clearly stated character-building value. The index at the back will help you quickly locate devotions specifically related to values you want to teach your child.

•Each devotion has six parts. . . .

 a) Look at God's Word—a simply-told Bible story

b) Memory verse—a short and easy-to-learn Bible verse.

c) Take a Closer Look—questions to make your child think about the value being examined.

d) Find the Hidden Secrets— an activity designed to child look inside him- or herself.

e) Discover for Yourself—an activity designed to make your child look to something or someone else for an answer.

f) Check with Your Guide—a short prayer to help build your child's relationship with God.

Whether you read these devotions to your child or your child reads them alone, each child will come to see how the Bible helps us in all phases of our lives. It is our guide. It is relevant to our everyday lives and will help us make right decisions.

We encourage you to make the Bible an interactive experience in your child's life. Start today!

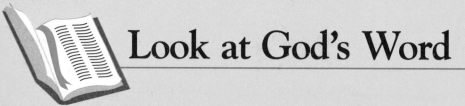

Look at God's Word

God's Wonderful World

Bible story from Genesis 1:6-13.

In the beginning, God lived, but there was nothing else. No people. No animals. No plants. No sun. No moon. No stars. No world. Nothing.

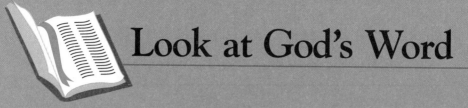

God Makes People

Bible story from Genesis 1:26—2:25.

God was ready to make someone very special. He wanted to make someone who could love Him. He wanted to make someone who could take care of the world.

So God made a man. He called the man Adam.

God put Adam in a garden. The garden was very beautiful.

Many trees grew there. A river flowed through it. Many animals lived there too.

The man ate food from the trees. He took care of the garden. God let him name the animals.

But Adam did not have a helper. There were no other people in the garden.

God said, "The man should not be alone. I will make him a helper." So God created a woman. He named the woman Eve.

The man and the woman could think. They could talk with God. They could be His friends.

God gave them food from the garden. He told them to take care of everything.

The man and woman were happy in the world God made for them.

Finally, God was done with His work. He looked at everything that He made. "I like it all," He said. Then He rested.

Memory Verse

I praise you because I am fearfully and wonderfully made.
Psalm 139:14

Value:
Praise

Take a Closer Look

Did you know that God saved the best for last?
God made the whole world, then He made man.
Why do you think God made man last? What special things
can you do that animals cannot?

Find the Hidden Secrets

God made you, too. He made you
special—not like anyone else.

When were you born?_____ .
Now that was a special day!

What color are your eyes?_____.
 Isn't that amazing?

What wonderful color is your hair? _____ . Wow!

What special thing can you do?_____.
That's really amazing!

How wonderful and amazing you are. You are one of God's
favorite creations!

Discover for Yourself

Find a plain piece of paper and a pencil. Hold the pencil in the hand you write or color with. Place the other hand on the paper. Spread your fingers wide. Now take the pencil and trace around your hand. You can color the hand if you want. Copy today's memory verse on the paper. Put this picture on your wall or door to remind you how wonderfully God made you.

Check with Your Guide

Dear God, thank You for such a wonderful world. Thank You for making all the animals. Thank You for making men and women. And most of all, thank You for making me! Amen.

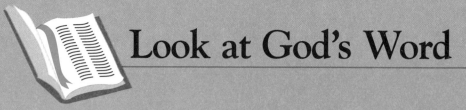

Noah Thanks God

Bible story from Genesis 8:1—9:17.

Noah and his family were in the ark for a long time. The animals were in the ark too.

It had rained for forty days and forty nights. When the rain finally stopped, water still covered the ground. The ark floated on the water. Then it came to rest on the top of a mountain.

Noah opened a window. All he could see was water.

Noah let a dove fly out of the ark. The bird came back with a leaf in its beak. "Trees are growing again," Noah said. "That means the water is lower."

Noah waited seven more days. Then he let the dove out again. This time the dove did not come back. It had found a dry home.

God told Noah, "You may leave the ark now. You can let all of the animals go find new homes." So he did.

"We obeyed God, and God kept us safe," Noah said to his family. Noah built an altar, and they all thanked God for keeping them safe.

God was happy. He liked what Noah did. God said, "I will make you a promise. There will always be spring and fall, summer and winter. But I will never send a great flood to cover the whole earth again."

Then God said, "I will make a rainbow in the sky. When you see the rainbow, remember my promise."

"Thank You, God," said Noah and his family. "Thank You for keeping us safe. Thank You for keeping the animals safe, too."

Memory Verse

*I can do everything
through Him who gives me strength.*
Philippians 4:13

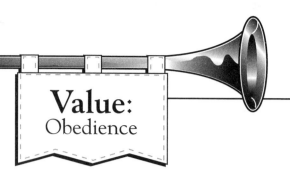

Value:
Obedience

Take a Closer Look

What would have happened if Noah had not obeyed God? Do you find it hard to obey your parents or teachers sometimes? Think of one thing you can do to obey your parents. Now, think of one thing you can do to obey God.

Find the Hidden Secrets

Connect the dots on the stripes of the rainbow. When you do, you will find places to obey God. On the blank stripe write one more place where you can obey God. Color the stripes with bright colors.

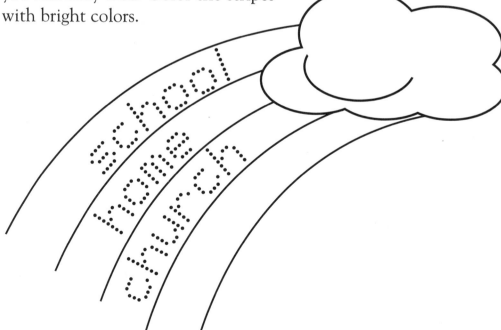

Discover for Yourself

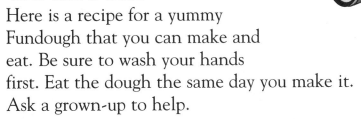

Here is a recipe for a yummy
Fundough that you can make and
eat. Be sure to wash your hands
first. Eat the dough the same day you make it.
Ask a grown-up to help.

Peanut Butter and Honey Fundough
> 1 cup peanut butter
> 1 cup honey
> 2 cups powdered milk

1. Mix all ingredients together in a bowl.
2. Add more powdered milk if needed to make moldable
   dough.
3. Form the dough into animal shapes. Make two of everything and pretend to be Noah guiding the animals on and
   off the ark.

Check with Your Guide

Thank You, God, for keeping Noah, his
family, and all of the animals safe. I'm so
glad Noah obeyed You. Thank You, God,
for helping me to obey You too. Amen.

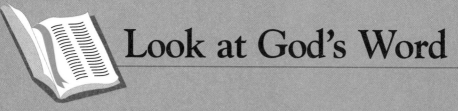

Look at God's Word

Abraham and Sarah Wait for God's Answer

Bible story from Genesis 15:1-5; 17:15-21;21:-1-3.

Year after year Abraham and Sarah prayed that God would give them a child. God promised to do it, but they had to wait. When they had waited a long time, they wondered, "Will God ever answer our prayer?"

One night God said, "Don't worry, Abraham."

God told Abraham to look at the night sky. "Try to count the stars," God said. "That's how many children and grandchildren

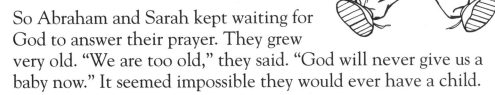

and great-grandchildren and great-great-grandchildren I will give you!" What a big family Abraham would have some day!

So Abraham and Sarah kept waiting for God to answer their prayer. They grew very old. "We are too old," they said. "God will never give us a baby now." It seemed impossible they would ever have a child.

Then one day God said, "Abraham, I am going to answer your prayer. You and Sarah are going to have a baby. You will name him Isaac."

Abraham and Sarah said, "We have prayed for so long, and we have waited a long, long time. Will God really give us a baby now when we are old?"

God answered their prayers. He gave them a baby boy! Abraham and Sarah named him Isaac which means "he laughs." That was a good name because baby Isaac made Abraham and Sarah laugh with joy.

How good God was to answer their prayer! And all the time they waited for His answer, God did not forget Abraham and Sarah. His answer finally came at just the right time.

Memory Verse

Wait for the Lord; be strong and take heart and wait for the Lord.
Psalm 27:14

Take a Closer Look

Have you ever waited a long time for something? Did it seem as if it would never happen?
Is there something special that you have asked God for?
What is it? God will answer your prayer at just the right time and in the right way.

 # Find the Hidden Secrets

God told Abraham that he would give him as many children as there are stars. That's a big family! How many stars you can draw on page 21?

Discover for Yourself

Abraham and Sarah named their baby boy Isaac, which means "he laughs." Your name is special too.
Ask your mom or dad why they chose your name. Ask them to help you find its meaning in a book about names.

 # Check with Your Guide

Dear God, help me to wait for an answer from You like Abraham did. Thank You for answering my prayers in special ways and at just the right time. Amen.

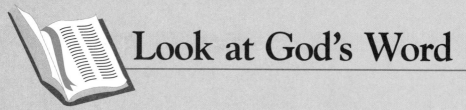
Jealous Brothers

Bible story from Genesis 37.

Joseph had ten older brothers and they were jealous of Joseph. Their father, Jacob, gave Joseph a new coat. This was a very special coat with long sleeves and many bright colors. Jacob had never given the older boys a coat that nice.

One night Joseph had a dream. He dreamed that he and his brothers each had a bundle of grain.

Joseph's bundle of grain stood up. But his brothers' bundles bowed down to Joseph's.

Joseph had another dream. The sun and moon and stars bowed down to him in that dream.

Joseph told his brothers about the dreams. The angry brothers said, "Do you think that someday you will be our king? We will never bow down to you."

One day the older brothers took their sheep to the hills to find green grass. Many days later Jacob said to Joseph, "Go see how your brothers are doing. Then come and tell me."

Joseph put on his beautiful coat and went to find his brothers. When his angry brothers saw him coming, they decided to get rid of him. They took off his coat and threw him into a deep, dry well.

Soon a group of men came by on camels. They were going to the land of Egypt to sell things.

One brother said, "Let's sell Joseph to these men. They will take him to Egypt and sell him as a slave."

So that is what the brothers did. They tore Joseph's beautiful coat and put goat's blood on it. When they got back home, they told their father, Jacob, "Oh, Dad, we found Joseph's coat. A wild animal must have killed him." This news made Jacob very sad.

Memory Verse

Make every effort to live in peace with all men.
Hebrews 12:14a

Take a Closer Look

What does it mean to be jealous? Joseph's brothers were jealous of him. Why? How did they treat Joseph?
Have you ever felt jealous of someone? How did you treat that person? It is very difficult to treat a person with love and kindness if you are jealous of him or her.

Find the Hidden Secrets

Joseph's brothers were jealous of the beautiful new coat that their father gave him. It had many wonderful colors. Draw a picture of Joseph's coat on page 25.

Discover for Yourself

Talk to a grown-up about something or someone that made him or her jealous. What did they do about it? Talk about how wanting something that someone else has keeps you from loving him or her. Ask the grown-up to pray with you about being jealous of others.

Check with Your Guide

Dear God, jealousy is such an awful thing. It makes it hard to love others. Help me to treat others with love and kindness. Amen.

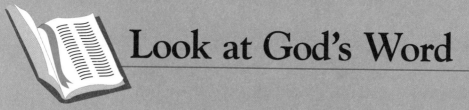

Look at God's Word

Miriam Does Her Part

Bible story from Exodus 1:1—2:10.

Miriam and her family were Hebrews. The Hebrews were God's people, and they lived in the land of Egypt. One day the king of Egypt said, "There are too many Hebrew people in my land. All the Hebrew baby boys should be killed."

Miriam had a baby brother. She wanted to do her part to help hide him from the king's men.

Miriam watched her mother make a basket bed for the baby. It was like a little boat. Then she and her mother put the baby into the basket and closed the lid.

"We will hide the baby in the weeds that grow along the river," Miriam's mother said. "That way when he cries, no one will hear him. I want you to hide in the weeds too, so you can keep your brother safe."

Soon Miriam saw some women coming to the river. It was the princess and her helpers. The princess was the king's daughter.

As the princess and her helpers walked by the place where Miriam and the baby were hiding, the baby started to cry. "What's that noise?" the princess asked. "It sounds like a baby."

One of her helpers found the basket and brought it to the princess. When the princess opened the basket, she saw the crying baby and picked him up. "It's a Hebrew baby boy!" she said. "I will adopt him and call him Moses."

Miriam ran to the princess and said, "I know someone who can help you take care of this baby."

"Good," the princess said. "Go get this woman." So Miriam ran to get her mother. Miriam was happy to help find her brother a safe new home.

Memory Verse

Do not forget to do good and share with others.
Hebrews 13:16a

Take a Closer Look

Miriam had a really important job to do for her
family. Each person in your family has an important job too.
Which person in your family fixes dinner? Which person reads
you a story? What do you do to help your family?

Find the Hidden Secrets

You have a very special family. Draw a
picture of your family.

Discover for Yourself

Show a grown-up the picture you drew of your
family. Talk about the special things each family
member does.

Check with Your Guide

Dear God, thank You for my family. We
each have a special job. Help me to do
my part. Amen.

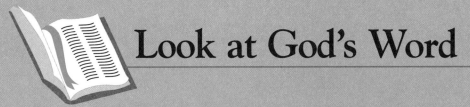

Look at God's Word

God Gives Moses a Helper

Bible story from Exodus 3:1—4:20.

When Moses grew up, he did not live with the Hebrew people in Egypt where they were slaves. Moses left Egypt and became a shepherd. One day while Moses was with his sheep, he saw a bush that was on fire. But as he watched the bush, he noticed it was not burning up.

Moses walked closer to the bush to look at it. Then he heard a voice call from the bush, "Moses, Moses! I am your God, Moses. I have seen the pain of My people, the Hebrews. Go back to Egypt and tell the king to let My people go free. I have a new land for them to live in."

"How can I make the king let the Hebrew people go?" Moses asked God.

"Don't worry. I will be with you to help," said God.

But Moses was still afraid. He asked, "What shall I tell the Hebrew people?"

God answered, "Tell them that I sent you."

Moses was still afraid to do what God asked. "Send someone else," he said. "I do not talk very well."

God answered, "I made your mouth, Moses. I will help you talk. But I will send your brother Aaron with you to do this hard thing."

So Moses went back to Egypt and found his brother Aaron. He was happy that God had given him a helper. And he was happy that God would be helping them too.

Memory Verse

Carry each other's burdens.
Galatians 6:2a

Take a Closer Look

God had a special message for Moses. He wanted Moses to tell the king to let His people go free. Moses was afraid. He thought the job that God had asked him to do was too hard.

What would be a hard job for you to do? Can you think of someone who has helped you do something hard? Thank the Lord for that person.

Find the Hidden Secrets

Draw a bush like Moses saw. Use a red crayon to color fire around the bush. Now use a yellow crayon to color over the red color. What color is the fire now?

Discover for Yourself

The memory verse today says to "Carry each other's burdens." This might mean that you could help someone carry a box or something heavy. But it can mean other things too. What would you do if you saw someone sad? How could you help that person? What can you do if you see your mother cleaning the house? By helping people, you carry their heavy loads or burdens. Aaron helped Moses carry his burden by speaking to the Hebrews when Moses was too scared. Look for ways to help others carry their heavy loads today.

Check with Your Guide

Thank You, God, for helping me to do things that are hard. Show me how I can help others. Amen.

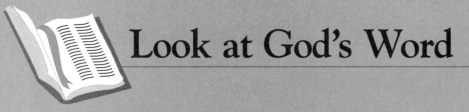
Look at God's Word

God Rescues His People

Bible story from Exodus 13:17—15:21.

When Moses and the Hebrew people left Egypt, they did not know the way to the new land God promised them. But they knew God would lead them. They knew nothing was too hard for God.

God sent a big cloud to lead His people in the daytime. At night the cloud glowed like fire and gave them light to see by.

The people followed the cloud. Soon they came to the Red Sea. They put up tents to rest there.

A story about
Trust

But then the people heard sounds. It was the Egyptian army! The king had sent his men to make the Hebrews go back to Egypt.

The Hebrew people were afraid when they saw the Egyptians coming. The Red Sea was in front of them, and they had no boats they could use to cross it.

"Do not be afraid," said Moses. "God will keep us safe." He knew nothing was too hard for God.

Then God said to Moses, "Hold up your shepherd's rod."

Moses did what God told him. Then God made the wind blow. It moved the water of the Red Sea. Soon there was a dry path through the sea. The people gathered their belongings and walked across.

The Egyptian army followed behind. But when the Hebrew people were safe, God made the water come back again. The Egyptians drowned in the sea.

Then the Hebrew people sang to God, "You are a great God. Nothing is too hard for our God."

Memory Verse

For nothing is impossible with God.
Luke 1:37

Value:
Trust

Take a Closer Look

God sent the wind to part the sea just at the right moment. Think of a bad problem you or your family may have had (someone lost his or her job, someone became sick, etc.). How did you solve your problem? Did you wonder if God would take care of you or your family? Do you have a problem right now that seems impossible? What is it? Ask God to help you.

Find the Hidden Secrets

Moses told the people not to be afraid. God would solve their problem. God can help you with your problem too. Draw a picture of how you will look after God helps you.

Discover for Yourself

Ask a parent or Sunday School teacher to tell you about a time when he or she faced a difficult situation. Ask how God helped to solve the problem. Tell him or her your memory verse from this story. Say it together.

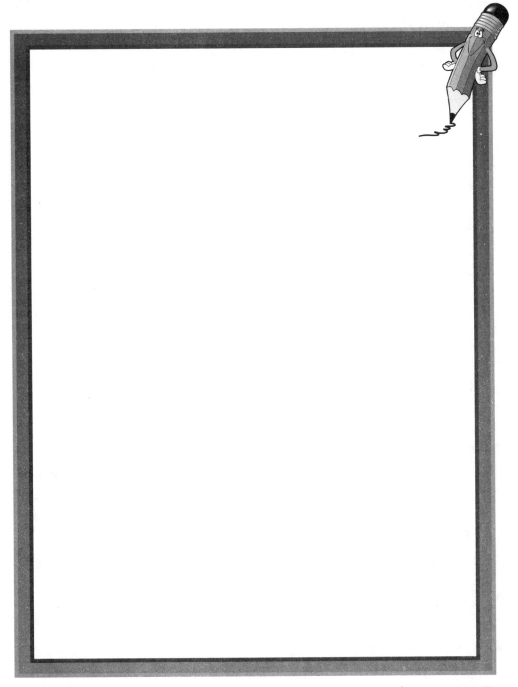

Check with Your Guide

God, You are really amazing. Nothing is impossible with You. Lord, when I am in trouble, help me remember how You split the Red Sea. Amen.

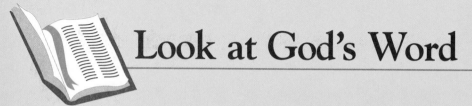

Look at God's Word

God Gives Rules to His People

Bible story from Exodus 19:1—20:20.

The Hebrew people put up tents and stayed near a big mountain. It was called Mount Sinai.

God spoke to Moses on the top of the mountain and gave him a message for the Hebrew people. "If these people will obey

Me," God said, "I will make them My special people. I will always help them."

Moses went down from the mountain. He told the Hebrew people God's words.

38

"We will obey God," the people told Moses. So Moses went up the mountain again to tell God that the people wanted to obey Him.

God said, "Tell My people to get ready. Soon they will meet Me." The people got ready to meet God just as He told them to do.

Then God came down on the mountain. The people heard His thunder and saw His lightning and they were afraid. They also heard a very loud trumpet and saw a big cloud on the mountaintop.

Then God called Moses up to the mountain again. He gave Moses rules for the people. God said, "I am your God. Love Me. I am the only true God. Worship Me, not things. Use My name the right way. Keep My day very special. Honor your parents. Do not kill people. Love your own husband or wife.

"Do not steal. Do not tell lies. Do not want what belongs to others."

Then Moses told the people not to be afraid. He said, "God wants you to obey His rules. They will help you love God and others."

Memory Verse

If you love me, you will obey what I command.
John 14:15

Take a Closer Look

Can you name two rules that God gave His people? Why are rules good? What would happen if we had no rules? How can we show God we love Him?

Find the Hidden Secrets

God wrote His rules on tablets made of stone. Draw two tablets here. Write one rule you want to obey on these tablets.

Discover for Yourself

What are the rules in your family? Why are these rules good for your family? Make a poster about these rules. Draw a picture of yourself obeying one of your family rules.

Check with Your Guide

Your rules are good, Lord. Your rules help me to love You and others. Help me to obey Your rules. Amen.

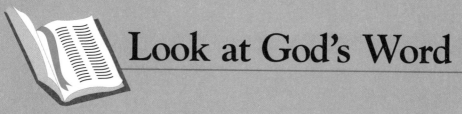

God Wins a Battle

Bible story from Joshua 5:13—6:27.

Joshua and the Hebrew people came into the new land of Canaan. They found out that most of the people living there were their enemies.

The great city of Jericho was near the Jordan River. It had high, stone walls all around it. The king of Jericho was not happy to see the Hebrews coming. "We will fight them if they get too close," he told his soldiers.

Joshua knew that Jericho was an enemy city. God told him, "You will have to fight the people of Jericho, but do not be afraid. I will help you win the battle."

God gave Joshua a special battle plan, and Joshua told the people. They were to march around the walls of Jericho without talking. Four priests would carry the ark while other priests blew horns. The Hebrew people did what God said.

The people marched around the city for six days. Each day they walked around the city one time. Then they went back to their camp. This was just what God had told them to do.

On the seventh day the people marched again. But this time they went around the city seven times.

The last time around, the priests blew their horns. Then all of the people shouted and the city walls fell down.

The people went into the city and took it from their enemies. God showed the people how to win the battle. They won because they did what He said.

Memory Verse

I will instruct you and teach you in the way you should go.
Psalm 32:8a

Value:
Obedience

Take a Closer Look

Why did the Hebrew people win the battle at Jericho? What did God tell Joshua to do? What do you think might have happened if Joshua and the people had not obeyed God? What happens when you don't obey your parents?

Find the Hidden Secrets

God guides us and tells us what we must do. He has a very special way of giving us His instructions. Cross out every lower case letter to find out where we can go to find God's instructions.

TkHmnEc
BehIoqBwxLagE

Discover for Yourself

Pretend that you are Joshua marching around Jericho. Build a wall out of blocks or boxes. Make a trumpet out of a paper towel tube, a funnel, or your hands. March around the wall six times. On the seventh time blow your trumpet really loud. Gently kick your wall and watch it tumble down.

Check with Your Guide

Dear God, Your directions are very important. Thank You for the Bible that guides me. If I obey Your directions in the Bible, I can win battles. Amen.

Draw a picture of your Bible here.

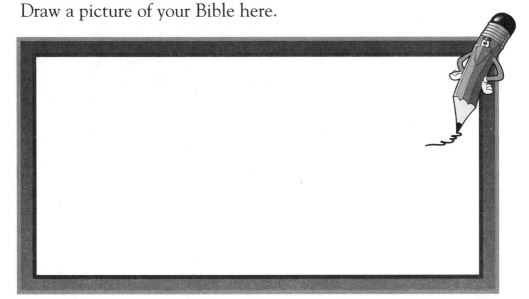

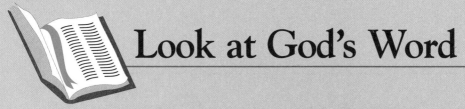

Ruth Honors Naomi

Bible story from the Book of Ruth.

Ruth and Naomi started off on a long trip. They were going to the place where Naomi had been born. Naomi had left her home many years before with her husband and sons. Now Naomi's husband was dead. Her sons were dead too. She had only Ruth to help her. Ruth had been the wife of one of Naomi's sons. Ruth loved Naomi as her own mother.

As they walked along, Naomi said to Ruth, "You don't need to leave your home to go on this trip with me."

Ruth hugged Naomi and told her, "I want to stay with you and help you. Your family will be my family. And your God will be my God."

Naomi and Ruth came to the end of their journey. Naomi's old friends were surprised to see her. They were glad she had Ruth to take care of her.

Ruth and Naomi were too poor to buy food. Ruth went to a field of grain. She picked up the leftover grain from the ground so she and Naomi could use it to make flour for bread.

Boaz owned the field of grain. Boaz saw Ruth and told her, "You may take all the grain you need because you are so kind to Naomi."

One day, Naomi told Ruth to ask Boaz for his help, so Ruth did. Boaz wanted to help Naomi and Ruth because he loved Ruth.

Ruth loved Boaz too. Ruth and Boaz got married. They asked Naomi to live with them so they could take care of her. Later, Ruth and Boaz had a baby.

Naomi's friends said to her, "God has been good to you. He has given you a fine family."

Memory Verse

Honor your father and your mother.
Exodus 20:12a

Value:
Respect

Take a Closer Look

What does the word *honor* mean? It means to
show love and respect for someone. Ruth showed honor for
Naomi by picking grain for food and taking care of Naomi.
Do you show honor to anyone? Who? How can you show that
you honor this person?

Find the Hidden Secrets

Check the boxes below that show how you
can honor your mother or father.

☐ I can put away my clothes.

☐ I can do my chores without complaining

☐ I can break my toys.

☐ I can tell others thank you when they do something for me.

☐ I can come when I am called.

Discover for Yourself

Make a card telling your parents how much you love and honor them.
You will need paper and crayons. Fold the paper in half. Now write on the front: THANK YOU FOR TAKING CARE OF ME. You can draw a pretty picture on the front if you want.

Inside write, I LOVE YOU! Then sign your name. Draw a picture inside too. Give the card to your parents or a special person whom you honor.

Check with Your Guide

Dear Lord, help me to honor those who love and care for me. Show me how to love and help them. Amen.

Look at God's Word

Samuel Listens

Bible story from I Samuel 3:1-19.

Samuel was a young boy. He lived in God's house and helped Eli, the priest. One night when Samuel was in bed, he heard a voice call his name. "Samuel, Samuel," the voice said.

Samuel ran to Eli. "Here I am. You called me?" asked Samuel.

The old priest said, "I didn't call you. Go back to bed, Samuel." So Samuel went back to bed.

Again the voice called, "Samuel, Samuel." *It must be Eli*, Samuel thought. He ran to Eli again. But no, Eli had not called him.

When the voice called a third time and Samuel ran to him, Eli knew it was God calling Samuel's name. Eli told Samuel, "Next time, tell God you will listen to what He tells you."

Samuel went to bed. Again God called him. Samuel said, "I'm listening, God." Samuel listened to everything God said. And Samuel kept on listening to God and obeying Him as he grew up.

Memory Verse

I will listen to what God the Lord will say.
Psalm 85:8a

Take a Closer Look

Have you ever missed something special because you were not listening to your parents or a teacher?
Samuel heard God's voice because Eli helped him be ready to do what God said.
What things might God want you to do? Are you ready to do what God says?

Find the Hidden Secrets

Hidden in this puzzle are three ways that you can listen to God. Can you find these words?

HEART
EARS
BIBLE

Draw a circle around each word as you find it. Hint: Some of the words read across. Some read up and down.

H	T	U	W	T	B
E	A	R	S	O	I
A	A	T	K	L	B
R	G	H	I	J	L
T	B	A	R	T	E

Discover for Yourself

Today you can play a game called "Telephone." Ask a grown-up or your brother or sister to play this game with you. The more people you ask to play the more fun it will be.

Have everyone sit in a circle. Whisper something in the ear of the person sitting on your left. Then that person should whisper the message to the person on his or her left. If just one person is playing with you, he or she will repeat it back in your ear. See if it comes back to you in the same words you said the first time or if the words have changed. Practice listening so you will be ready to hear God.

Check with Your Guide

Dear God, I'm so glad You speak to me. Help me to be ready when You call me to help You. Amen.

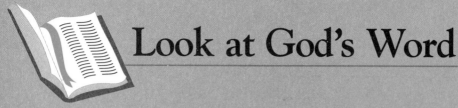 # Look at God's Word

David Fights a Giant

Bible story from I Samuel 17.

David's older brothers were soldiers in the army of God's people. They went to fight an enemy army. David watched his father's sheep. He kept them safe from lions and bears.

One day David's father told him, "Take some food to your brothers."

When David found his brothers, they weren't fighting the enemy. All of the soldiers were afraid!

"What is the matter?" David asked.

"You'll see," his brothers said.

Soon an enemy soldier walked out. He was a giant named Goliath. "I want a man to fight me!" he shouted to the army of God's people. But none of the soldiers moved.

David said to the soldiers, "We should not be afraid of this giant. God is on our side. He will help us."

King Saul heard about the brave young man. He sent for David. "You are just a boy," King Saul said.

"I will fight the giant," David said. "God helped me kill a lion and a bear. I know He will help me kill this giant."

David picked up five stones for his sling. Then he went out to meet Goliath. The giant had a sword and a spear.

Goliath laughed when he saw David. "You are just a boy!" said Goliath.

David said, "You are brave because of your sword and spear. But I am brave because I trust God."

David put a stone in his sling. He pulled back the sling and let it go. The stone flew out of the sling and hit the giant in the head. Goliath fell down dead.

Then the soldiers chased away the enemy army. David had shown them how to be brave. David trusted God to help him.

MAP

X

Memory Verse

The Lord is my helper. I will not be afraid.
Hebrews 13:6b

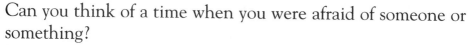

Value:
Trust

Take a Closer Look

Do you think David was afraid of Goliath?
Can you think of a time when you were afraid of someone or something?
Do you have a GIANT problem that you can trust God to help you with?

Find the Hidden Secrets

Draw a picture of Goliath. Then draw a picture of David. Goliath was a much bigger man than David and could have easily beaten him in battle. But David trusted in God. God is bigger than any problem we face.

Discover for Yourself

You will need a blank piece of paper, a pencil or a marker, glue, and five small rocks. Ask a grown-up to help you if you need help. Write the memory verse at the top of the paper. Now glue the rocks on the paper. Beside each rock, write down something that you are afraid of. Then ask God to help you not to be afraid of the things you wrote down.

Check with Your Guide

Dear God, You are bigger than any giant or problem. Help me not to be afraid. Help me to trust You as David did. Amen.

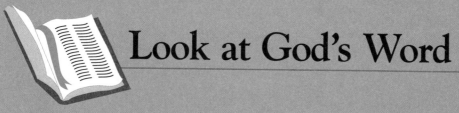

David's Psalm

Bible story from Psalm 145:1-12.

David wrote many songs. They were called psalms. As a young boy, David wrote these songs as he watched his father's sheep. When he grew up and became king, he wrote more psalms praising God. These psalms were like letters from David to God.

This is one of King David's psalms:

I will tell everyone how great You are, my God and King. Every day I will thank You. I will praise You forever and ever. You are worthy of praise. You are greater than anything else.

People should tell their children and their children's children the mighty things You do. I will tell everyone how great You are! Everyone will sing of Your goodness.

You are loving and forgiving. You are slow to get angry. You are good to everyone. All Your people will give You thanks. Everyone will know how great You are and how wonderful Your kingdom is.

Memory Verse

Great is the Lord and most worthy of praise.
Psalm 145:3a

Take a Closer Look

Why should we give God praise? What are some ways we can give or show praise to God?

David loved to write songs about God. What is your favorite song about God? Sing it.

Find the Hidden Secrets

Who can you tell about the wonderful things God has done? Draw a picture of yourself telling that person about God.

Discover for Yourself

Make a poster of things for which you praise God. You can draw pictures or cut them from old magazines to glue on your poster. Include things like pictures of your family, pictures of God's creation, food, and clothing—anything you are thankful that God made. Put it up so your whole family can praise God with you.

Check with Your Guide

Dear God, You are so wonderful. You are worthy of praise! I praise You for the world You made. I praise You for my family. I praise You for loving me! Amen.

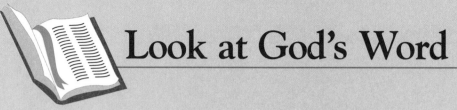

Look at God's Word

King Solomon's Request

Bible story from I Kings 1:32-40; 2:12; 3:3-15.

King David was very old. A new king was needed for God's
people. So Solomon, David's son, was anointed king.

But Solomon was worried. Would he be able to rule well? He knew he needed God's help.

God talked to Solomon in a dream: "Ask Me for anything you want."

Solomon knew what he wanted. "Lord, please give me wisdom to be a good king," he said.

God was pleased with Solomon. "You could have asked to be rich. You could have asked for a long life. But you asked for the best thing. I will give you wisdom. I will also make you rich. And if you keep obeying Me, you will have a long life, too."

Memory Verse

If any of you lacks wisdom, he should ask God . . .
and it will be given to him.
James 1:5

Take a Closer Look

If you could have anything in the whole world, what would it be? Think carefully.

Who gave you your mind? How can you use your mind to help God?

 # Find the Hidden Secrets

Solomon used his wisdom to be a good king. God helped Solomon make wise decisions. Draw a picture of how God's wisdom can help you to be a good kid.

Discover for Yourself

On a blank piece of paper write, GOD HELP ME TO HAVE A WISE MIND. Put the paper where you can see it during the day. Notice when you do or think something wise. Maybe you decide to pick up your toys without being told. That's wise! Or, you remember to say thank you. That's a really smart thing to do. Every time you do something wise, tell God thank You for giving you wisdom.

Check with Your Guide

Dear God, please give me a wise mind. Help me to use my mind to help You and others. Amen.

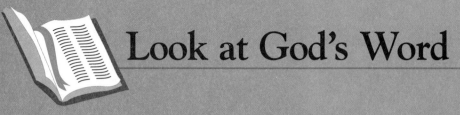

Look at God's Word

Naaman Gets Help from a Servant Girl

Bible story from II Kings 5:1-15.

Naaman was the leader of a big army. But Naaman was sick with leprosy. No doctors knew how to help him get well.

A girl who worked as a servant in Naaman's house wanted to help. She told Naaman's wife, "My master should go and talk to God's prophet, Elisha. God will show Elisha how to help my master."

When Naaman heard the girl's idea, he asked his king if he could go to see Elisha. The king wanted Naaman to get well too, so he sent a letter to the king of Elisha's country. The letter said, "Please make Naaman well."

Elisha heard about the letter. He sent a message to the king that said, "Send Naaman to me." But when Naaman got to Elisha's house, Elisha wouldn't come out to see him. Instead, Elisha sent his servant outside to give Naaman a message.

Elisha's message said, "Go wash in the Jordan River seven times and God will make you well."

Naaman was angry. This was no way for Elisha to treat an important man like him! But Naaman's servants said, "Please do what Elisha says."

So Naaman went to the muddy Jordan River. He dipped himself in the water once, twice, three times, four times; but nothing happened.

Naaman dipped himself in the water five, six, seven times. And when he came up for the seventh time, the leprosy was gone. He was well!

Naaman went back to thank Elisha. He said, "Now I know that your God is the only true God." Naaman thanked God for making him well and for the servant girl who told him God could help.

Memory Verse

Serve one another in love.
Galatians 5:13b

Value:
Helpfulness

Take a Closer Look

Many people don't know that God can help them. Do you know someone like that? How can you tell them about God?

Find the Hidden Secrets

Naaman didn't think dipping in muddy water would heal him, but it worked! Draw a picture of Naaman washing in the Jordan River.

Discover for Yourself

Think of someone you know that has a BIG problem. Maybe they are sick, or maybe they have lost something really important to them. How can you help? What could you say to help them know that God loves them? Pray and ask God to give you just the right words.

Check with Your Guide

Dear God, thank You for always helping me. Help me to tell others that you can help them too. Amen.

Look at God's Word

Worshiping at God's House

Bible story from II Chronicles 29:20—30:27.

When Hezekiah became king, it bothered him that his people didn't care about worshiping God. King Hezekiah said to the

people, "It is wrong for us to forget about God. Let's gather together and worship Him."

So everyone went to the temple and worshiped. The people

prayed, "Dear God, we are sorry for doing wrong things. We promise to learn about You and to praise You."

Then King Hezekiah and his people worshiped God with music. Some played musical instruments like harps, trumpet, and cymbals. Some of the people sang songs to worship God. They sang words like: "Shout for joy to the Lord, all the earth. Serve the Lord with gladness; come before Him with joyful songs. Give thanks to Him and praise His name."

Later, King Hezekiah sent letters to all his people who lived far away. He told them to come and worship at God's house too.

Many people came to the temple. They also asked God to forgive them for doing wrong things, and they sang songs and played music. The priests read from God's Word and told the people about God. Then the people gave God their offerings and prayers.

King Hezekiah and his people worshiped at God's house for seven days. It was such a happy time that they didn't want to go home. So they worshiped God for seven more days. God was pleased that His people had come to the temple to worship Him.

Memory Verse

Worship the Lord with gladness;
come before Him with joyful songs.
Psalm 100:2

71

Value:
Worship

Take a Closer Look

The story told us that the people worshiped at God's house for seven days. What things did King Hezekiah and the people do to worship God?

What is your favorite thing about going to God's house? What things do you do to worship God at church? Draw a picture of you worshipping God.

Find the Hidden Secrets

Sometimes it's hard to get ready for Sunday worship. Families often run around trying to find their things and end up arguing. When this happens, it's hard to go to worship with songs of joy.

Here is a list of things you can do to get ready to worship God at church. Add some ideas of your own.

The night before:
- [ ] Lay out the clothes you want to wear to worship.
- [ ] Put your Bible where you can easily find it.
- [ ] Lay out your coat and anything else you might need.
- [ ] Go to bed early.
- [ ] Pray at bedtime, thanking God for being able to worship Him.
- [ ] _____

Sunday morning:
- [ ] Get up right away.
- [ ] Get dressed, comb your hair, and brush your teeth.
- [ ] Eat a good breakfast.
- [ ] Don't fight or complain.
- [ ] Pray that God will help you to worship Him.
- [ ] _____

Discover for Yourself

Make your own special musical instrument called a Water Glass Xylophone. Ask a grown-up to help you get eight empty water glasses and line them up in a row. Tap the first glass gently with a spoon. Now get a pitcher of water. Pour a little water into the second glass. Tap it with the spoon. Does it sound different than the first glass? Pour a little water in the third glass and a little more in the fourth glass. Put a little more water in each glass than you did the one before it. Fill the last glass all the way to the top. Tap each glass with a spoon and see how they sound. Now you're ready to play your xylophone and sing a joyful song to the Lord.

Check with Your Guide

God, help us to prepare to worship You. Thank You, God, that we can worship You. Thank You that we can sing songs of joy and praise. Amen.

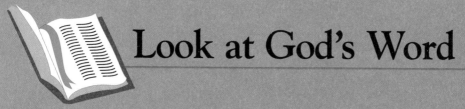

Look at God's Word

Three Brave Men Show Faith in God

Bible story from Daniel 3.

A long, long time ago, King Nebuchadnezzar built a shiny gold idol. It was ninety feet high and nine feet wide.

Then he sent word throughout the land that all leaders should worship the idol. When the music played, the leaders bowed and worshipped the statue . . . all except Shadrach, Meshach, and Abednego. They refused to bow before the idol.

The three men said, "We will not bow down. The God we serve said, 'Don't worship anything but Me!' And He is able to help us no matter what you do."

King Nebuchadnezzar grew very angry. He ordered his soldiers to throw the three men into a fiery furnace!

Immediately, the king's order was carried out. Then an amazing thing happened. When the king looked inside, he saw the men walking around! Their clothes were not burned. They were not hurt in any way.

"Didn't we tie three men up and throw them into the fire?" the king asked. "Look, I see four men walking around."

The king shouted, "Shadrach, Meshach, and Abednego, come out! Your God has saved you!"

"I'm giving an order," the king said. "No one can say anything against the God of Shadrach, Meshach, and Abednego. No other god can save people the way their God can."

Memory Verse

You shall have no other gods before me.
Exodus 20:3

75

Value:
Commitment

Take a Closer Look

Has anyone ever made fun of you for believing in God? What did you do?

What are ways that you can show God that He is important to you?

Find the Hidden Secrets

Here is a special way of using crayons. You will need yellow, red, orange, and black crayons. First color one part of the space on page 77 yellow. Take the red and do the same to another part of the space. Color the rest of the space orange. Now, take the black crayon and cover all the colors. Cover the entire space with black. With the blunt end of a pen or the handle of a spoon, carefully draw four men by scratching through the black crayon. Don't press too hard. You will see the men standing in the furnace unharmed.

Discover for Yourself

The memory verse tells us not to put any gods before the Lord. A god doesn't have to be an idol made of stone, wood, or gold. It can be anything you make more important than God. Is there anything you like more than God? Do you have a favorite super hero on television? Do you think more about him than God? Ask a grown-up to pray with you not to make anything more important than God.

Check with Your Guide

Dear God, You are more important than anyone or anything in the whole world. Help me to love You more than anything else. Amen.

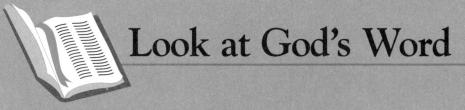

Look at God's Word

Daniel Obeys God

Bible story from Daniel 6.

Daniel loved God and prayed to Him three times each day. He also worked hard for the king. He was a trusted servant, so King Darius wanted to put Daniel in charge of the whole kingdom.

But the other leaders were jealous and wanted to get Daniel in trouble. "Make a law," they told the king, "that no one can pray except to you for thirty days."

The king thought this sounded fine so he signed the law with his royal pen. Anyone who did not obey would be thrown into the den of lions'.

But Daniel went home and did as he always did. He prayed to God. Nothing could stop him from obeying God's law. His enemies heard him and reported Daniel to the king.

The king was sad that these crafty men saw Daniel breaking the law. But even the king couldn't change the law, so Daniel was thrown into the lions' den.

The king said, "Daniel, God be with you." He didn't know what else to do. All night he wondered, "Is Daniel all right?" Early in the morning, he went to check the den.

"Did God take care of you?" he asked. How glad he was when Daniel replied, "God sent His angel to shut the lions' mouths. I am not hurt."

The king was filled with joy. "Get Daniel out of the den," he said. "Daniel's God is the One to whom we should pray. He saved Daniel from the lions."

Memory Verse

Do what is right and good in the Lord's sight.
Deuteronomy 6:18a

Value:
Faithfulness

Take a Closer Look

Has a friend ever asked you to do something you knew was wrong? Did you follow your friend or did you decide to do what was right? What happened? How do you feel when someone asks you to do wrong things?

Find the Hidden Secrets

Let's make a picture of hungry lion using an ink stamp pad. Press your thumb on the ink pad and then press it on the space below. If you don't have a washable ink pad, watercolors paints will work. Dampen your thumb and press it on your favorite watercolor. Now press your thumb on page 81. Repeat, making another thumb print right below the top one. Now draw ears, whiskers, a face, a curly mane, and a tail on your thumb print. Pretend the Lord shut the mouth of your lion.

Discover for Yourself

The Bible is a book that tells us lots of ways to obey God and make right choices. Ask a grown-up to help you think of ways that you can obey God. Make a list of those ways on a separate piece of paper.

Check with Your Guide

Dear God, sometimes it is hard to do what is right. Help me choose to obey You. Amen.

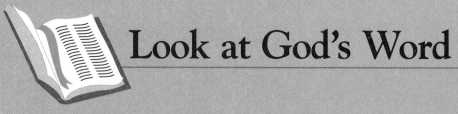

Esther Saves Her People

Bible story from the Book of Esther.

King Xerxes, the ruler of Persia, was looking for a wife to be his queen. The most beautiful girls in the land were being called to the palace to meet him.

One of these girls was Esther, Mordecai's cousin. She had lived with Mordecai since she was a little girl. Mordecai knew that the king would love Esther because she was very beautiful and kind. When the time came to select a queen, Esther was the one chosen.

"Don't tell the king you are a Hebrew," Mordecai warned. "There are many people in this land who do not like us because we worship the one true God."

One day Mordecai heard that a man named Haman was planning to have all of God's people killed. He tricked the king into signing a law, making it okay on one special day to kill God's people and steal the things they owned.

Mordecai put on torn clothes and ashes to show he was upset. When Esther heard what he had done, she sent a man to ask him what was wrong. Mordecai said, "Go to the king and tell him about Haman. See if the king can help us. Even you, Esther, won't be safe if Haman's plans work out. He must be stopped."

Esther was afraid. She knew that even the queen couldn't see the king without being invited. If he was unhappy that she came, he could have her put to death. So Esther prayed three days for courage. Then she went to see the king.

King Xerxes was surprised to see his wife. The king raised his scepter to show Esther that she was welcome to speak to him.

"My Lord," Esther said with a bow, "I would like to invite you and Haman to have dinner with me."

The king agreed and so he and Haman enjoyed having dinner with Esther. And when she asked, they both agreed to come to dinner again. The next time they came, Esther told the king about Haman's plan to kill all the Hebrews in the kingdom, including herself.

The king was very angry. He made a new law to help save God's people. Then he had Haman hanged. With God's help, Queen Esther had saved her people.

Memory Verse

Our God is a God who saves.
Psalm 68:20a

Value:
Courage

Take a Closer Look

How do you feel when you face a big problem? Esther was afraid when she had a big problem. What was the first thing she did? What can you do when you have a problem?

Find the Hidden Secrets

On one side of the space below, draw a picture of a problem you have had before. In the space on page 85, draw a picture of how God helped you solve the problem.

Discover for Yourself

Think of a big problem you have. Maybe you are scared of your neighbor's dog, or maybe you have to clean up a really big mess. How can you face the problem one little step at a time? Ask a grown-up to help you think of ways to solve your problem. Write down your plan.

Problem:

Steps to Solve this Problem: 1. _____
2. _____
3. _____

Check with Your Guide

Dear Lord, thank You for helping me when I have a problem. Knowing You gives me courage and makes me feel brave. Amen.

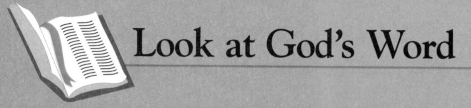

Look at God's Word

Jonah and the Big Fish

Bible story from Jonah 1-3.

One day God told a man named Jonah to go to the city of Nineveh. Jonah was a preacher. God wanted him to preach to the people of Nineveh and tell them that God was unhappy with the wrong things they were doing.

That's too hard, thought Jonah. *I don't want to go to Nineveh. Those people are our enemies.* So he found a boat that would take him far away, as far away from Nineveh as he could get.

But after the boat headed out to sea, a big storm came up. The thunder rumbled and crackled. The lightning flashed. Even the sailors were afraid. They started to throw things off the boat to make it lighter. But nothing helped.

The captain went to find Jonah. "I know you are a preacher. Ask your God to save us!" he said.

Then Jonah said, "Throw me into the sea and the storm will stop. This trouble is my fault." Jonah knew that God had sent the storm because he was running away from what God wanted him to do.

So the sailors threw Jonah into the sea. And he went down, down, down into the dark, cold water. But Jonah didn't die. God sent a big fish to save him. The big fish opened its mouth and swallowed Jonah in one big gulp.

Jonah stayed inside the fish's belly for three days. It was dark and smelly and very uncomfortable, but Jonah was happy. He was still alive!

Jonah thought about what had happened. He knew that God had saved him, so Jonah prayed. He thanked God for saving his life. He told God he was sorry for running away. And he told God he would obey Him and go to Nineveh.

After three days, God had the big fish swim close to land and spit Jonah onto the shore.

Then God said, "Jonah, obey Me and go to Nineveh. Tell the people there what I said."

So Jonah obeyed God and went to Nineveh. The people there listened to what he had to say. They told God they were sorry for the wrong things they had done and God forgave them.

Jonah learned an important lesson. He learned that you can't run away from God. Obeying God makes life a lot happier. Jonah was thankful that God forgave him and gave him a second chance to obey.

Memory Verse

I desire to do your will, O my God; your law is within my heart.
Psalm 40:8

Take a Closer Look

Can you think of a time when you didn't want to obey your parents? What did you do? Do you ever pretend not to hear your mother or father calling you? Why?
Why is it good to obey?

Find the Hidden Secrets

In the space on page 89, draw a picture of a BIG fish. Then draw Jonah inside the big fish.

Discover for Yourself

Ask your mom for five index cards or cut some pieces of paper the size of index cards. Draw a fish on one side of each card. Now ask your mom or dad to write on the other side of each card one thing you need to focus on so that you will learn to obey better (come the first time your are called, do chores without complaining, etc.). Each day this week read one card and work on being more obedient in that way.

Check with Your Guide

God, sometimes I can be really stubborn. I don't always obey You or my parents the way I know I should. Help me to be obedient. Amen.

The Angel's Message

Bible story from Luke 1:26-56.

Mary was a young woman who lived in a town called Nazareth. One day an angel came to give Mary a message from God.

At first Mary was afraid. But the angel said, "Do not be afraid. God is going to do something wonderful for you. You will have a baby boy. And you will name Him Jesus. Jesus will be the Son of God."

"Even your cousin Elizabeth is going to have a baby in her old age," the angel continued. "Nothing is impossible with God!"

"I believe your message," said Mary. "I will do what God wants me to do."

Mary hurried to tell her cousin Elizabeth the angel's message. God helped Elizabeth know that Mary's baby would be the Savior of all people.

"Blessed are you, Mary," Elizabeth said as they greeted one another. "And blessed is the baby that you are going to have."

Then Mary sang a song of praise to God. She thanked God for all the wonderful things He does. She thanked God for sending His Son, Jesus, to be the Savior.

Memory Verse
I tell you the truth, he who believes has everlasting life.
John 6:47

Value:
Faith

Take a Closer Look

Have you ever heard something you didn't believe was true? What was it? Did it turn out to be true?

Find the Hidden Secrets

The angel told Mary to name her baby boy Jesus. All the words or phrases below describe Jesus. Choose five that start with each of the letters of His name. The first one is done for you.

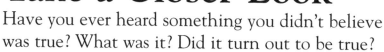

J <u>ehovah</u>

E _____

S _____

U _____

S _____

Jehovah, Understanding, Emanuel, Joyful,
Savior, Loving, Son of God, Wonderful

Discover for Yourself

Mary believed the special message from
the angel. Who told you that Jesus is the Son
of God? Ask your dad or mom why he or she believes Jesus is
the Son of God?
Look for the angel's message in the story. Then fill in the
blanks below.

The Angel's Message:

1. "D__ n__t __e a__ra__d."
2. "Y__u wi__ __ ha__e a
   __a__y b__y."
3. "An__ __o__ wi__ __ __am__
   Hi__ __es__s."
4. "J__s__s __ill __e t__e
   __on o__ G__d."

Check with Your Guide

Dear God, Thank You for sending Jesus, Your Son.
Help me to believe everything Jesus said in the Bible.
Amen.

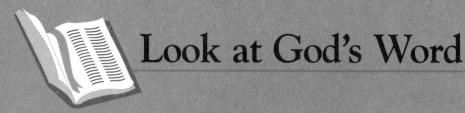

Look at God's Word

The Shepherds' News

Bible story from Luke 2:1-20.

Mary and Joseph were on their way to a town called Bethlehem. The ruler of the land had made a law that said all people should go to their hometown to be counted. It was a hard trip for Mary. She was going to have a baby. God's Son would soon be born.

When Mary and Joseph got to Bethlehem, the town was full of people. There was no room for Mary and Joseph to stay in the inn.

Mary and Joseph went to stay in a stable. Soon Mary's baby was born. Mary wrapped the baby in strips of cloth. She made a bed for Him in a manger. The baby's name was Jesus.

That same night some shepherds were watching their sheep in the hills near Bethlehem. Suddenly, the shepherds saw an angel. A bright light was shining around the angel. The shepherds were afraid.

The angel said, "Do not be afraid. I have wonderful news! It is happy news for everyone. Our Savior has been born in Bethlehem. He is Christ the Lord. Go to Bethlehem and find Him. He is wrapped in strips of cloth. You will find Him lying in a manger."

Then there were many angels in the sky. All of them were singing praises to God for sending Jesus the Savior. Then they went back to heaven.

The shepherds hurried to Bethlehem. They wanted to see the Savior. After the shepherds saw Jesus, they praised God for sending His Son. They told everyone they saw that Jesus the Savior had been born.

Memory Verse

Today in the town of David a Savior has been born to you.
Luke 2:11a

Take a Closer Look

What was the wonderful news that the shepherds heard?
How do you feel when you get some exciting news? What do
you do?

Find the Hidden Secrets

Draw and color a picture on page 97 of what
the shepherds saw when they came to the
stable in Bethlehem.

Discover for Yourself

The shepherds ran out and told everyone that
they had seen Jesus. Pretend you are one of the shepherds. What would you tell someone about the baby
Jesus? Act out this story for a younger child or grown-up.

Check with Your Guide

Dear God, The story of the baby Jesus is wonderful news. Thank You for sending a Savior to
love us. Help me to tell others the Good News
about Jesus. Amen.

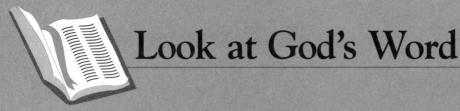

Look at God's Word

Young Jesus at the Temple

Bible story from Luke 2:41-52.

Mary and Joseph lived far from the temple, so they only went there once a year.

When Jesus was twelve years old, He went with Mary and Joseph to the temple. They had to walk almost a week. Many other people walked with them. The people were glad to get to Jerusalem. They could see the temple right away. It was a beautiful place.

Jesus went to the temple with His family. They worshiped God at the temple. They sang and prayed to God. They gave their offerings to God.

Then Mary and Joseph started back home. They walked all day. They thought Jesus was safe with another family in their group.

That night Mary and Joseph looked around. But they couldn't find Jesus. They said, "We must go back to Jerusalem."

They went back to look for Jesus. They found Him at the temple. Jesus was listening to wise teachers. He asked them some questions. And He answered their questions. Mary went over to Jesus, "Why have You done this to us? We have looked everywhere for You."

"Why did you look so hard?" asked Jesus. "Didn't you know I would be here? This is My Father's house." Jesus was talking about God. Jesus knew that God was His Father.

Jesus liked to be at God's house. But He obeyed Mary and Joseph. He went back to Nazareth with them.

God was pleased with Jesus. People were pleased with Jesus too.

Memory Verse

I rejoiced with those who said to me,
"Let us go to the house of the Lord."
Psalm 122:1

Value:
Self-discipline

Take a Closer Look

How can you get to know someone better?
Why did Jesus stay in the temple?
What are some ways you can spend time with God?

Find the Hidden Secrets

Jesus said that He would be in whose house? His _____.
Connect the dots of the matching letters to see whose house Jesus loved.

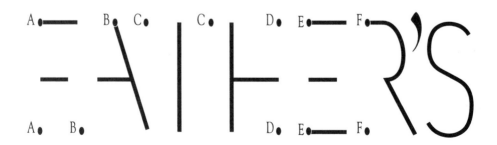

Discover for Yourself

Cut some pictures out of old magazines to
show what you think a father does. How does
God act like a father to us? Why is it important
to go to your heavenly Father's house, like Jesus. Show your
pictures to a grown-up. Glue one or two of your pictures in
the space below.

Check with Your Guide

Dear God, I love spending time with You. Teach
me more about You and the Bible. Thank You for
being my heavenly Father. Amen

Jesus Is Our Best Friend

Bible story from Matthew 19:13-15; Mark 10:13-16.

The crowds that followed Jesus weren't just grown-ups. Some children came to see Jesus too. Their families wanted Jesus to pray for the children and bless them.

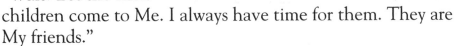

Jesus' helpers knew He was busy. "Leave Jesus alone," they said. "He is too busy with grown-ups. He doesn't have time for children."

The boys and girls were sad. But then they heard Jesus say, "Wait! Let the little children come to Me. I always have time for them. They are My friends."

Jesus smiled at the boys and girls. "God loves all boys and girls," Jesus told them. He put His arms around them, and they wiggled together to get close to Him.

He looked at the grown-ups and said, "The kingdom of heaven belongs to everyone who is like these children. Grown-ups must love God. They must believe in Me as children do."

Memory Verse

Let the little children come to me.
Mark 10:14b

Value:
Friendship

Take a Closer Look

What is a friend? What things do friends do for you? What things do you do for your friends? Draw a picture of your friend. Why is this friend special to you?

_____is my friend.

Find the Hidden Secrets

Jesus told grown-ups that to inherit the kingdom of heaven, they must become as little children. Little children are special friends to Jesus. Ask an adult for some ideas why Jesus would say this. How are adults different from children?

Discover for Yourself

Friends love to share things and have fun together. Make this bubble solution and share it with a friend. Ask a grown-up for help.

Big Bubbles

6 parts water
2 parts dishwashing liquid
(The best brand to use is Joy.)
3/4 part corn syrup

Mix all the ingredients together and store in a covered container. Have a grown-up cut off the top and bottom of a coffee can and hammer the inside edges smooth. Dip either end in the solution and wave through the air to make big bubbles.

Check with Your Guide

Dear Jesus, thank You for being my Friend. Help me to be a good friend to others. Amen.

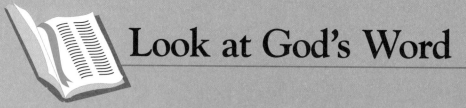

Look at God's Word

Jesus Stops a Storm

Bible story from Mark 4:35-41.

Jesus had been teaching by the shore of a lake all day. So many people had come to hear Him that He got into a boat. His

helpers rowed a short distance from the shore so the people could see and hear Jesus better.

When evening came, Jesus said to His helpers, "Let's go over to the other side of the lake."

The helpers started to row, and Jesus lay down in the boat and fell asleep. He was very tired from His long day of teaching the people.

Before they had gone far, the wind began to blow. It made the waves get bigger and bigger. Water began to splash into the boat. Jesus' helpers were afraid of the storm. They didn't know what to do. Everyone was sure the boat would sink.

"Wake up, Jesus!" the helpers called. "Teacher, don't You care if we drown?"

Jesus spoke. "Stop," He said to the wind. "Quiet! Be still!" He said to the waves. The wind stopped and the big waves became still.

Everything was quiet on the lake. Jesus looked at His helpers. "Why were you afraid?" Jesus asked them. "Don't you trust Me?"

The helpers saw Jesus' special power. "Even the wind and waves obey Him!" the helpers said.

Memory Verse

Do not let your hearts be troubled.
Trust in God; trust also in Me.
John 14:1

Value:
Trust

Take a Closer Look

Why did the winds and waves obey Jesus?
What kinds of things scare you?
What do you do when you are scared?

Find the Hidden Secrets

Draw a picture of something that REALLY scares you. Then, write the words "Trust in God" across the bottom of the space. Whenever you think of the thing you are afraid of, ask God to help you not be afraid. He can do anything!

Discover for Yourself

Make your own "storm on the sea." You
will need a large pan or bowl filled half way
with water, some white vinegar, baking soda,
and a small toy boat or floating toy. Pour 1/2 cup
of baking soda into the pan of water and stir until it dissolves.
Place the boat in the water so it floats. Now pour 2 table-
spoons of vinegar into the water. Watch what happens! Use
this to tell the story of how Jesus calmed the storm to a
younger child or a grown-up. You can repeat the action by
adding more vinegar or baking soda.

Check with Your Guide

Dear Lord, I am so glad that You have the
power to do anything. Thank You for taking
care of me when I am scared. Amen.

Look at God's Word

Jesus Uses a Boy's Lunch

Bible story from John 6:1-14.

Jesus wanted to talk to His helpers alone. So He took them up a hill, but soon many other people followed them. These people came from towns all around. They had seen Jesus make people well. They wanted to hear Him talk about God.

Jesus loved the people and wanted to help them. So He began to teach them about God.

After a while, it was time for supper, but there was no town close to them. The people began to get hungry.

Jesus talked to one of His helpers. "Philip, where can we buy food for all of these people?"

Philip said, "It would take too much money. We can't buy food for *all* the people. We should send them home."

Then Andrew came to Jesus. He was also one of Jesus' helpers.

Andrew said, "Here is a boy with a lunch he is willing to share. But he only has five small rolls of bread and two small fish. That won't be enough food for everyone. There are more than five thousand people here!"

Jesus said, "Have the people sit down on the grass." Then He thanked God for the food and broke the bread and fish into pieces.

Jesus' helpers passed out the pieces of bread and fish, and there was enough food for everyone!

When everyone was finished, Jesus told His helpers, "Gather the leftover food." So the helpers picked up the leftovers. They filled twelve baskets!

The people knew that Jesus was special. Now they saw more of His special power. With one little boy's lunch, Jesus fed more than five thousand people!

Memory Verse

So whether you eat or drink or whatever you do,
do it all for the glory of God.
I Corinthians 10:31

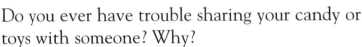

Value:
Sharing

Take a Closer Look

Do you ever have trouble sharing your candy or
toys with someone? Why?
Do you like it when someone shares with you?
Why is sharing good?

Find the Hidden Secrets

The boy had five rolls of bread and two small fish.
Yet one small lunch fed many, many people, and they had
twelve baskets full leftover! What a miracle Jesus did that day!
Draw a picture of some things you could share with others.

Discover for Yourself

Invite a friend over to your house for lunch. Ask
your mom to help you make two peanut butter and
jelly sandwiches. Ask your mom to slice an apple in five
pieces. Tell your friend about the boy who shared his lunch
with Jesus. Then share your lunch with your friend.

Check with Your Guide

Jesus, You are so special! What a neat miracle You
did! Thank You for teaching me how to share. Amen.

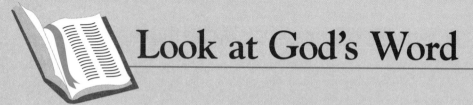

Look at God's Word

Two Builders

Bible story from Matthew 7:24-29.

This is the wise man who built his house on hard ground.

This is the foolish man who built his house on the sand.

One day Jesus told this story about two men.

A wise man built a house on hard ground. Then one night it rained and rained. The wind blew on the house too. But the wise man was safe because his house on the hard ground stood straight and strong.

A foolish man built a house too, but he built his house on the sand. Then one night there was a big storm. The wind blew and it rained hard.

The foolish man was not safe because his house was built on sand, and it soon fell down with a crash!

People who obey Jesus are like the wise man. They will be safe when problems come because they trust in Jesus.

People who do not obey Jesus will end up very sad because they trust in things that can't really help them. They are like the man whose house fell down.

Memory Verse

If you love me, you will obey what I command.
John 14:15

Take a Closer Look

Do you like to build things? What kinds of things do you build?

Every time you obey Jesus, you build your life stronger for Him. What kinds of things can you do to obey Jesus?

Find the Hidden Secrets

Circle the building blocks that will help you trust in Jesus.

Reading the Bible	Watching lots of television	
	Eating Candy Bars	Obeying your parents
Praying	Going to church	
		Reading comic books

Discover for Yourself

Build a tower using saltine or graham crackers. See how high you can make the tower without it falling. Now try it again, but this time spread peanut butter along the edges to make the crackers stick together. Which tower was the tallest and strongest? Praying, going to church, and reading the Bible work like the peanut butter in our lives. They help us grow strong in the Lord so we don't fall when tough storms come into our lives.

Check with Your Guide

Dear Jesus, help me to be like the wise man. I want to obey and trust You. Amen.

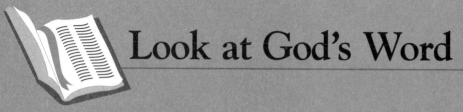

Look at God's Word

Keeping God's Day Holy

Bible story from Matthew 12:9-15; Exodus 20:8-11.

It was the sabbath day. God's commandment said the sabbath should be a holy day to worship Him. Jesus wanted to worship God. He was going to a place called a synagogue. This was where God's people went on the sabbath day to worship and learn about God.

The rulers of the synagogue did not like Jesus. "Let's see if Jesus breaks any of our rules for the sabbath. Then we can get Him in trouble," said one of rulers.

Another ruler pointed to a poor man with a crippled hand. "Maybe Jesus will heal that man's hand," he said. "That's against the rules. Healing the man would be work and no work is allowed on the sabbath."

The rulers went to Jesus and asked, "Is it right to heal someone on the sabbath day? Isn't that work?"

Jesus answered, "If one of your sheep fell in a hole on the sabbath, wouldn't you lift it out? A person is more important than a sheep. So it is right to do good on the sabbath."

Jesus said to the poor man with the crippled hand, "Put your hand out." The man put his hand out and suddenly, he could move his fingers and wave his hand. Jesus had healed him!

Jesus knew the right way to keep the sabbath day holy. He worshiped God. And He helped other people.

Memory Verse
Remember the Sabbath day by keeping it holy.
Exodus 20:8

Value:
Worship

Take a Closer Look

Is there one special day during the week that you and your family go to church or do special things for God? What day is it? What other kinds of things do you do on that day?
How can you make this day even more special?

Find the Hidden Secrets

Draw a picture on page 121 of what you and your family do on the Lord's special day.

Discover for Yourself

Ask a grown-up what the word *holy* means. Make a list of things that are holy and good that you can do on the Lord's special day. Now make a list of some things that you might not want to do on this day. The next Lord's day, take out your list and plan how you will make that day holy.

Check with Your Guide

Dear Jesus, thank You for showing how to make God's day special. Help me to worship God and help others on this day and every day! Amen.

121

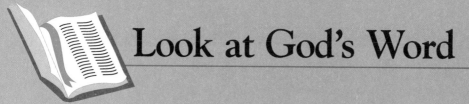

Look at God's Word

A Young Man Loves His Money

Bible story from Matthew 19:16-22; Exodus 20:3; Deuteronomy 6:5.

A rich young man asked Jesus a question. "Teacher, I want to live with God forever. What good thing should I do?"

Jesus said, "If you want to live, obey God's commandments."

"Which ones?" the rich man asked.

Jesus told him, "Do not kill. Do not steal. Do not lie. Honor your father and mother. And love your neighbor as much as you love yourself."

"I obey these commandments," the young man said. "What else must I do?"

Jesus said, "If you want to be perfect, sell what you own and give your money to poor people. Then your riches will be in heaven, and you can come and follow Me."

Jesus knew the man loved money more than he loved God. If the man gave his money away, he wouldn't have to think about it anymore or spend time deciding what to buy with it.

Jesus wanted him to give his money to the poor because the man had so much and the poor had so little. Giving his money away would show he loved God more than he loved his money.

The rich man didn't want to hear what Jesus said. He walked away. He loved his money too much to give it up—even to obey God.

Memory Verse
Love the Lord your God with all your heart.
Matthew 22:37a

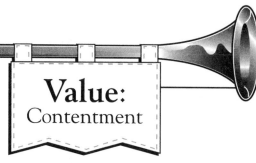

Value:
Contentment

Take a Closer Look

What are your favorite things? Make a list in the space below.

1. _____
2. _____
3. _____
4. _____
5. _____
6. _____

7. _____
8. _____
9. _____
10. _____
11. _____
12. _____

Of the things you've written down, which is the most important to you? Do you find that it is hard to share this thing with others? Why?

Find the Hidden Secrets

GOLD

The rich young man loved money more than God. Cross out the third letter in the heart to see what Jesus said we should love more than GOLD.

Discover for Yourself

What are some ways you could show God that He is important to you? Ask a grown-up to help you think of some ideas. Then draw a picture of one way you will show God that you love Him.

Check with Your Guide

Dear God, I want to love You with all my heart. Please show me the things that I love more than You. Help me to give these things up. Amen.

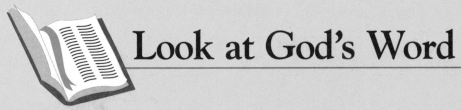

Look at God's Word

The Good Samaritan

Bible story from Luke 10:30-37.

Jesus often used stories to teach people what God wanted them to do. One day He told this story.

A Jewish man was walking along a lonely road. Some robbers were hiding behind the rocks. They jumped out and hit the man many times until he was almost dead. Then they took his money and clothes and left him lying by the road.

Soon a priest from God's temple came walking by. He saw the hurt man, but he did not stop to help.

Next a Levite from the temple walked past. The Levite saw the hurt man, but he walked on by too.

Then a Samaritan man walked by. The Samaritans and the Jews did not like each other. But the Samaritan man still stopped to help the hurt Jewish man.

The Samaritan washed the man's sores and put the man on his donkey. Then the Samaritan took the hurt man to an inn where the man could rest and get better. In the morning when the Samaritan went on his way, he gave the owner of the inn some money.

"Take care of this hurt man until I come back," the Samaritan told the owner.

After Jesus told this story, He asked, "Who was a kind neighbor?"

"The one who helped the man," said a listener.

Then Jesus said, "I want you to be a kind neighbor to everyone you meet too!"

Memory Verse
Love your neighbor as yourself.
Luke 10:27b

Value:
Helpfulness

Take a Closer Look

The Samaritans did not like the Jews. Is there
someone that you don't like very much?
How can you love people you do not like?
What kinds of things do you do to take care of yourself?
How can you love others in the same way?

 # Find the Hidden Secrets

Draw a picture on page 129 of one way you can show
love to someone you have a hard time liking.

Discover for Yourself

The Samaritan did not live in the same neigh-
borhood as the Jewish man. They didn't even know
each other. Yet, Jesus said they were neighbors. Make a
list of people who you might call your "neighbor." Maybe
they live right next door. Or maybe they work at the place
where your mom buys groceries. Don't forget to write down
people you might not like. How can you show love to these
neighbors?

 # Check with Your Guide

Dear Jesus, thank You for the story of the Good
Samaritan. Help me to love people even if I don't
like them very much. Amen.

129

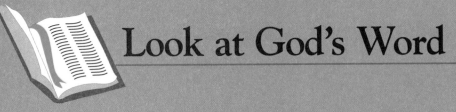

A Sorry Son Goes Home

Bible story from Luke 15:1, 2, 11-24.

Jesus told this story to show how God forgives people who are sorry for their sins.

Once there was a father with two sons. The younger son wanted to leave home. He asked his father for his share of the family's money. Then he packed his clothes and left home. The boy's father was sad to see him go. He knew his son was not wise. And he was afraid his son would get into trouble.

The young man walked and walked. He came to a place where no one knew him. He spent his money on all kinds of things that weren't good for him. Soon his money was all gone.

The young man went to work for a farmer. He fed the farmer's pigs. Sometimes the young man was so hungry, he wanted to eat the pigs' food. The young man was sorry he had left his father. He was sorry he had done bad things.

My father's servants have good food to eat, he thought. *I will go home to my father and tell him I'm sorry for things I've done. Maybe he will let me be one of his servants.*

So the young man left his job with the pigs. He walked and walked and walked. Then finally he saw his house in the distance. Someone was standing in front of it. It was his father. When his father saw him coming, his father ran to meet him.

The boy was thrilled to see his father, and his father was thrilled to see him.

The son said, "Father, I have done wrong. I am not good enough to be your son. May I be one of your servants?"

"No, you are my son. I forgive you." Then the father said to his servants, "Bring some good clothes and shoes for my son. And prepare lots of food. Let's have a party. My son is sorry for what he has done, and now he has come home!"

Memory Verse
You are forgiving and good, O Lord.
Psalm 86:5a

Value:
Forgiveness

Take a Closer Look

Have you ever done something you thought could not be forgiven? What was it?

If you do something wrong, what should you do?

How do you think God feels when you disobey Him?

Find the Hidden Secrets

Write a letter telling God that you are sorry for something you did wrong.

Thank Him for forgiving you.

Dear God,

_____

_____

_____

_____

_____

_____

_____

Signed:_____

Discover for Yourself

In the story, the son did not just tell his father he was sorry. He also showed him he was sorry by wanting to serve his father. Ask a grown-up how you can show God that you are sorry for what you wrote about in your letter. Draw a picture of yourself putting your words into action!

Check with Your Guide

Dear God, You are so forgiving. When I do things that are wrong, You always forgive me. Help me to show You with my actions that I'm sorry. Amen.

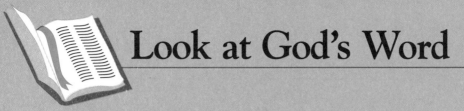

Zacchaeus Is Sorry

Bible story from Luke 19:1-10.

Zacchaeus was a tax collector, but he wasn't honest. He made people pay too much tax money. Then he kept some of the money for himself. This made Zacchaeus rich, but he did not have many friends.

Zacchaeus heard Jesus was coming to town. Everyone was talking about the great stories Jesus told and the wonderful things He did for people. So Zacchaeus wanted to see Jesus too.

When someone cried, "Jesus is coming!" a great crowd of people went out to meet Him. Everyone in town wanted to see Jesus. Zacchaeus was very short. He could not see over all the people. So Zacchaeus climbed up a tree beside the road and waited.

Soon Jesus came walking by the tree. Jesus stopped and looked up. He saw Zacchaeus and said to him, "Come down from that tree! I am coming to your house for a visit today!"

Zacchaeus climbed down right away. He led Jesus to his house. The other people were surprised. "Jesus is going to visit the home of a bad man," they said.

But Zacchaeus was sorry he had been bad. He let Jesus know how sorry he was. "I will give half of everything I have to poor people," said Zacchaeus. "And I have taken too much tax money from some people. So I will pay them back four times as much."

Jesus was happy to hear what Zacchaeus had to say. Jesus knew Zacchaeus was really sorry for all the things he had done wrong. He said to Zacchaeus, "I came to help people like you."

Memory Verse

*If we confess our sins, he is faithful and just
and will forgive us our sins.*
I John 1:9a

Value:
Repentance

Take a Closer Look

If you were Zacchaeus, would you have climbed a
tree to see Jesus?

Do you think it was hard for Zacchaeus to admit he had done
wrong things? Do you find it hard to admit that you have
done something wrong? Why?

What can you do to show you are really sorry for your sins?

Find the
Hidden Secrets

Think of something that you need to tell
God that you are sorry for doing. Draw a
picture of how you can show God you are sorry for something
you did wrong.

Discover for Yourself

Zacchaeus not only told Jesus he was sorry, he told
everyone else he was sorry too. Think of one person
that you can tell you are sorry for something you did
wrong. Now think of ways you can show you are sorry. Maybe
your mom told you to clean your room and you didn't do it.
How can you show her you're sorry? Maybe you didn't share
your toys with your brother or sister. What could you do now?

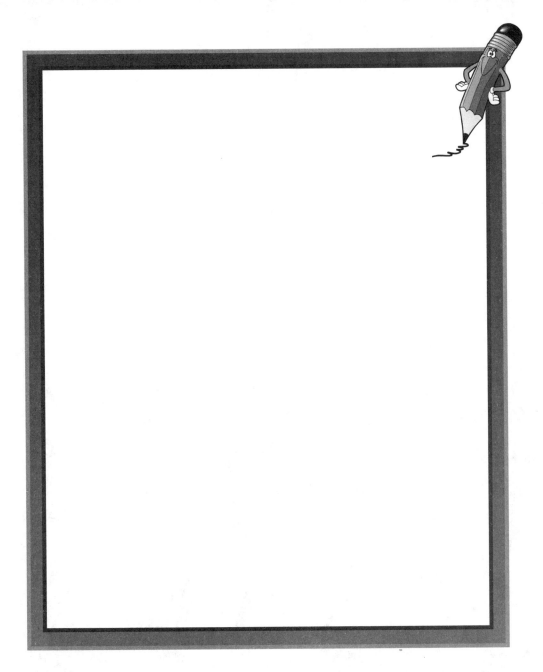

Check with Your Guide

Dear Jesus, You are so wonderful and forgiving.
Help me to say I am sorry when I do wrong things.
Help me to tell and show others I'm sorry. Amen.

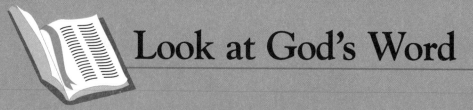

Jesus, the King and Savior

Bible story from Luke 19:29-40; 22:39-42.

Jesus and His helpers were going to Jerusalem. Jesus told two of His helpers to go into a small town near the city.

"You will find a donkey tied up there. Bring it to Me," said Jesus. "Someone may ask you why you are taking the donkey. Tell him that the Lord needs it."

The helpers found the donkey. They said that the Lord needed it. Then they took it to Jesus.

Some helpers put their coats on the donkey's back. Jesus rode the donkey to Jerusalem.

As Jesus went along, people laid their coats and palm branches on the dirt road in front of Him. They did this to show Jesus that they wanted Him to be their new king.

Many people began to shout, "Hosanna! Jesus is our king! He comes in the name of God!" The people waved palm branches as He passed by them.

Some men in the crowd said to Jesus, "Make the people stop shouting and singing."

"No," said Jesus. "Let them shout and sing their songs of praise."

A few nights later Jesus went to a garden where he liked to go to pray. His helpers went with Him, but they soon fell asleep. So Jesus prayed all alone.

Jesus said to God, "Father, I know You want Me to die to save people from their sins. It will be a very hard thing. But I'll do what You want Me to do. I will be the Savior."

Very soon after that, Jesus did die. The Savior died and then God raised Him from the dead so that we can be in God's family.

Memory Verse

How good it is to sing praises to our God.
Psalms 147:1b

Take a Closer Look

The people called Jesus their king. How would you treat a king?

Why is Jesus also called "The Savior?" What does a savior do for his people? What did Jesus do to become our Savior?

Find the Hidden Secrets

Draw a picture of what you think King Jesus might look like. Now draw a picture of you giving praise to Jesus. He is our king and our savior. What are some other ways that we can show praise to Jesus?

Discover for Yourself

Ask your mom if you can tear a small branch from a tree in your yard. (If she says no, cut a piece of newspaper to look like a large leaf. Cut approximately one inch strips toward the center from the outside edge, being careful not to cut all the way through. Affix the "palm leaf" to a fly swatter, badminton racket, or dowel stick with tape.) Wave it in the air. Go into your yard and pretend that you are welcoming Jesus to your home. Dance and sing "Hosanna! Jesus is our king!" Isn't praising Jesus exciting?

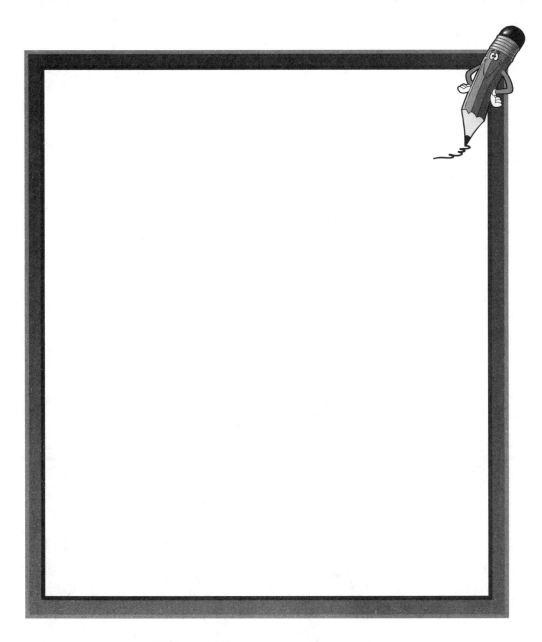

Check with Your Guide

Jesus, You are such a wonderful king. Thank You for also being my Savior. I will praise You with my whole heart and shout, "Hosanna! You are my king!" Amen.

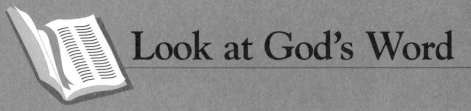

Jesus Died for Us

Bible story from Mark 15:1-39; I Corinthians 15:3.

Jesus, the only Son of God, came to tell others about His Father. But not everyone wanted to hear what He had to say. Some people even hated Jesus. They had Him arrested and brought before Pilate, the governor. "Are You a king?" Pilate asked Jesus.

Jesus said, "Yes, what you say is true."

A story about
Forgiveness

This made Jesus' enemies very angry. They told lies and said bad things about Him, but Jesus was quiet.

Pilate knew Jesus had done nothing wrong. Pilate said to the people, "This is a special holiday. I can let one prisoner out of jail. Shall I let Jesus go? Or shall I let Barabbas go?" Barabbas was a killer.

"Let Barabbas go! Kill Jesus!" the people yelled.

"What has Jesus done?" asked Pilate.

The people just yelled louder, "Kill Jesus! Put Him on a cross!"

Pilate wasn't happy about what the people wanted, but he had his soldiers take Jesus away. They nailed Jesus to a wooden cross. The people stood around and watched and laughed. "Come down if You are so great," the people yelled.

Jesus could have come down. He could have called an angel army to help, but He stayed on the cross until He died. That was what God, His Father, had asked Him to do.

God asked Jesus to die to take the punishment for everyone's sins. Because Jesus died on the cross, God promises to forgive people's sins and let them be in His special family.

When Jesus died on the cross, a soldier said, "Jesus really was the Son of God!"

Memory Verse
Christ died for our sins.
I Corinthians 15:3b

143

Take a Closer Look

Have you ever gotten into trouble for something
someone else did wrong? What happened? How did you feel?
Jesus took the blame for the things that we have done wrong.
What would happen if Jesus had not died for us?

Find the
Hidden Secrets

Jesus died on the cross so we could be in God's
family. In the space beside the drawing of the cross, write
today's memory verse. Color the cross.

Discover for
Yourself

Cut a piece of cardboard or drawing paper in
the shape of a cross. On the cross, draw a picture
of things in your life for which Jesus died, such as
disobeying your parents, taking something that doesn't
belong to you, or not telling the truth. Ask a grown-up to
help you think of other things. Hang this cross where you can
see it often. When you look at it, thank Jesus for dying on the
cross for you.

_____ _____

_____ _____ _____

I Corinthians 15:3b

Check with Your Guide

Dear Jesus, You did nothing wrong, but You died on the cross anyway. Thank You for dying for me. Please forgive me for the wrong things I've done. Amen.

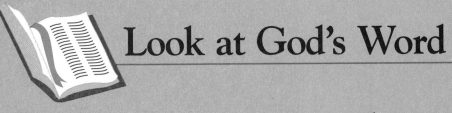

Look at God's Word

Mary Shares Good News

Bible story from Luke 23:33; John 20:1-18.

Mary was very sad. Jesus had died on a cross. Now it was early Sunday morning. Mary and some other women were going to Jesus' tomb.

When they got there, the big stone in front of the tomb had been rolled away!

The tomb was open. Jesus' body was not there!

Mary ran to tell Peter and John. "Jesus' body is gone!" she cried. "He is not in the tomb."

Peter and John ran to the tomb. John got there first. But he didn't go inside until Peter got there. Peter and John saw that Jesus was gone. But they didn't know where He was. So they went away from the tomb.

Mary went to the tomb again. She began to cry. She looked inside the tomb and saw two angels.

"Why are you crying?" the angels asked. "They have taken Jesus," Mary said. "I don't know where they have put Him."

Then Mary turned and saw someone. He was standing near the tomb. She thought it was the gardener. He said, "Why are you crying? Who is it you are looking for?"

Mary said, "Sir, if you took Jesus away, please tell me where you put Him."

"Mary," the man said.

Mary saw that it was Jesus. Jesus was alive! "Teacher!" Mary said.

Mary was not sad anymore. She went to Jesus' friends. What good news she had to tell them! "I have seen Jesus," said Mary. "Jesus is alive!"

Memory Verse

He is not here; he has risen, just as he said.
Matthew 28:6a

147

Take a Closer Look

How would you have felt if you had found the tomb empty?
Do you think you would have been happy to see Jesus alive?

Find the Hidden Secrets

Mary was very surprised to find Jesus gone from the
tomb. Draw a picture of the empty tomb and the
angels inside.

Discover for Yourself

Pretend you are Mary or Peter or John. First act
out how you felt when Jesus died. Then pretend to
find the empty tomb. Now how would you act when
you found out Jesus was alive? Act out the story for a younger
child or grown-up to tell them the good news of Jesus coming
back to life.

Check with Your Guide

Jesus, You said that You would come back
to life and You did! Thank You for not
staying in the tomb. You are alive just as
You promised to be. Amen.

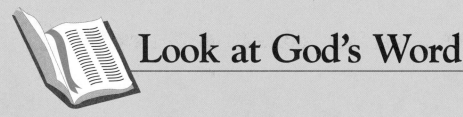

Look at God's Word

Jesus Goes to Heaven

Bible story from Luke 24:50-53; Acts 1:8-14.

Jesus died and came alive again. Many people saw Jesus after He came back to life. He spent time with His helpers teaching them the things they needed to know before He went away.

One day Jesus took His helpers for a walk up a big hill.

When they came to the top, Jesus stopped and said, "Wait for God's Holy Spirit. He will help you be My witnesses. Go and tell other people about Me. Tell people here. Tell people in other lands. Tell people all over the world."

As the helpers stood there listening to Jesus, He began to rise up off the ground! Soon He was so high in the sky that a cloud covered Him. Jesus' helpers didn't know what to think. They just stood there looking up into the sky.

Suddenly two angels dressed all in white were beside them. "Why are you looking up into the sky?" the angels asked. "Jesus has gone up to heaven. You saw Him go. He will come back someday in the same way."

Then Jesus' friends went back to the city. They prayed together and waited for the Special Helper Jesus promised to send them.

"Thank You, God, for sending Jesus," the friends prayed. "Thank You for making Jesus alive again. Help us do what You want. We will work for You until Jesus comes back."

Memory Verse

I will come back and take you to be with me. . . .
John 14:3b

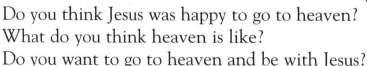

Value:
Faith

Take a Closer Look

Do you think Jesus was happy to go to heaven?
What do you think heaven is like?
Do you want to go to heaven and be with Jesus?

Find the Hidden Secrets

The disciples watched Jesus go up into the clouds.
On page 153, draw a picture of Jesus in the clouds.

Discover for Yourself

Go outside and look up in the sky. Look for some
clouds. Think about what it would have been like to
watch Jesus go to heaven. As you watch the clouds, tell
Jesus you are happy that He is alive. Thank Him that He will
come back again someday. Promise to work hard telling others
about Him.

Check with Your Guide

Dear Jesus, I know it must be wonderful in heaven.
Thank You for the promise that You will come back
again someday. Amen.

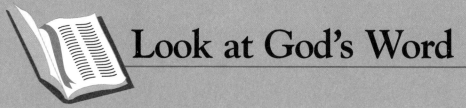

Look at God's Word

Christians Give an Offering

Bible story from Acts 11:22-30.

Paul and Barnabas went to a church in a town called Antioch. There they taught the people about Jesus from God's Word.

One day a message came from the church in Jerusalem. It said, "A famine is coming. Soon it will be hard to grow food. The people in the church of Jerusalem will not have enough food."

The Christians in Antioch said, "We want to help the church in Jerusalem. They helped us by sending Paul and Barnabas to teach us about Jesus. We will help them have food to eat."

So the people in Antioch took an offering. They sent the money to the church in Jerusalem.

The people in the Jerusalem church were very happy to get the money. They said to Paul and Barnabas, "We are glad for the Christians at Antioch! We are thankful for their help. Now we can buy food to eat."

Memory Verse

God loves a cheerful giver.
II Corinthians 9:7b

Take a Closer Look

Why were the people in Antioch happy to help the church in Jerusalem?

Have you ever helped someone because you thought you had to help them? Do you think it is more fun when you want to help someone? Why?

Find the Hidden Secrets

Pretend you are a Christian in Antioch. You have just heard that people are starving in Jerusalem. On page 157, draw a picture of how you can help.

Discover for Yourself

Ask a grown-up if they know of someone who needs help. Maybe a family in your church is going through a hard time. Think of ways you can help them. Can you give them some food? Do you have some clothes or toys you could share? Pray and ask God how you can help.

Check with Your Guide

Dear God, You have helped me so many times. Show me how to help others. Help me to be a cheerful giver. Amen.

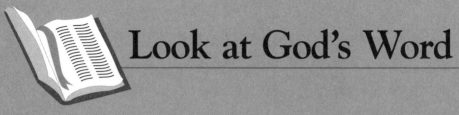

Paul Helps a Church

Bible story from Acts 18:1-11.

Paul travelled to many places telling people about Jesus. One day he went to the city of Corinth. There he met Aquila and his wife, Priscilla, who were also followers of Jesus.

Aquila and Priscilla were tentmakers like Paul. They made tents and purses and other useful things. So when Paul went to visit them, he decided to stay and work with them.

Every Sabbath Paul went out to tell people about Jesus. Paul wanted people to believe in Jesus and become part of God's church. But as time went by, Paul began spending all of his time teaching people about Jesus. Many people believed in Jesus.

Some people did not like what Paul had to say. They said mean things to Paul and threatened to take action against him.

"If you will not listen to what I have to say," Paul said, "I will go to people who want to hear about Jesus."

One night Jesus talked to Paul in a vision. He said, "Keep on teaching the people about Me. I will be with you."

So Paul kept on preaching and the church kept on growing. Paul helped many people grow to be like Jesus.

Memory Verse

Serve the Lord with all your heart.
I Samuel 12:20b

Take a Closer Look

Are there lots of churches where you live? Right after Jesus went to heaven there were not many churches. Why do you think it might have been hard to start a new church? How could you help your church grow?

 # Find the Hidden Secrets

Draw a picture of one way you can help your church.

Discover for Yourself

There are lots of ways you can help your church. You could volunteer to help clean up your Sunday School classroom. Maybe you could pass out song books or help new kids find the right classroom. Think of someone you could ask to come to church with you. Practice what you will say with your mom or dad. And, the most important thing you can do is pray for your church.

 # Check with Your Guide

Dear God, Thank You for my church. It is a place where I can learn about You and have friends that love You too. Help my pastor as he teaches us about You. Show me how to help my church. Amen.

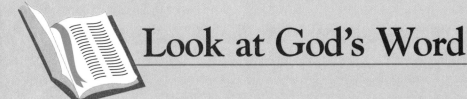

Look at God's Word

Timothy Learns God's Word

Bible story from II Timothy 1:1-5; 3:14-17.

Timothy was a little boy when he first learned about God. His mother and his grandmother taught little Timothy from God's Word, the Scriptures.

"Pay attention, Timothy," said his mother. "God will teach you in the Scriptures what is right and what is wrong."

"Pay attention, Timothy," said his grandmother. "The Scriptures tell us what God is like. He loves us and wants us to obey Him."

Timothy paid attention when his mother and grandmother told him stories from Scripture. As Timothy grew older he learned to read the Scriptures too. But most important, Timothy learned to love God. And because he loved God, Timothy wanted to do the things that pleased God.

Timothy learned from the Scriptures that God didn't want him to steal and lie. Timothy tried not to do these things. Timothy also learned that God wanted him to forgive people and share the things God gave him. Timothy tried to do these things.

One day, when Timothy was a young man, Paul came to Timothy's town. Paul said, "Jesus is God's Son. The Scriptures said that God would send Jesus. God wants you to believe in Jesus."

Timothy's mother said, "I will believe in Jesus."

Timothy said, "I will believe in Jesus."

Some time later, Paul came back and talked to Timothy. "Timothy, you know the Scriptures well. You would be a good helper for me. We will teach people what the Scriptures say about Jesus. We will teach people to love and obey Jesus."

Timothy was glad he had paid attention when his family taught him God's Word. All that he learned helped him be a good worker for God.

Memory Verse

I have set my heart on your laws.
Psalm 119:30b

Take a Closer Look

Timothy's mother and grandmother taught
him the Scriptures. Who teaches you the Bible?
Name something you remember learning from the Bible.
Paul asked Timothy to be his helper. What would you have
done if you were Timothy?

Find the Hidden Secrets

What is your favorite story or lesson in the Bible.
Draw a picture of it on page 165.

Discover for Yourself

You will need a blank piece of paper and markers
or crayons. At the top of the paper, write today's memory verse. Below the verse, draw pictures of the people
who teach you God's Word—your parents, grandparents, the
pastor at your church, your Sunday School teacher and anyone who has taught you the Scriptures. Thank the Lord for
these people. Ask God to help them teach you God's Word.

Check with Your Guide

Dear God, I love Your Word. It is full of wonderful
stories and lessons. Thank You for the people who
teach me the Bible. Help me to always obey Your
Word. Amen.

List of Values

Each devotion in this book illustrates at least one character value that you will want your child to develop. The story and activities reinforce the learning process. You will want to use this quick reference list for those special teaching moments when you want to share information on a specific value.

You will also want to see...

The Children's
DISCOVERY BIBLE

Discovering God's Word for the First Time

Your child will delight in this new children's Bible from ChariotVictor. With over 150 stories from the Old and New Testaments, your child will be captivated by the action and excitement of learning about God and His Word.

The text is simple and specially crafted by Christian educators with decades of experience in sharing the Bible with young children. Each word is carefully chosen to communicate both the Bible story and the Christian value it teaches. And each story is followed by a simple memory verse to plant God's Word in your child's heart.

In an art style made popular by today's movie animators, Still Animation Artwork makes the Bible fun for children today. Each illustration will make the Bible come alive to your child.

Discover God's Word for the first time!

Read to Me: Ages 3-6
Read it Myself: Ages 5-8

ChariotVICTOR
PUBLISHING
A DIVISION OF COOK COMMUNICATIONS